matisse
at villa
le rêve

matisse

at villa

le rêve

1943–1948

Marie-France Boyer

with photographs by
Hélène Adant

Thames & Hudson

For Rupert and Thomas, who made this delightful voyage possible.
For Nigel and his books, companions from the first day.

Concept and research by Marie-France Boyer
Designed by Michael Tighe
Translated from the French by Anna Bennett

First published in 2004 in hardcover in the United States of America by
Thames & Hudson Inc., 500 Fifth Avenue, New York, New York 10110

thamesandhudsonusa.com

ISBN 0-500-51175-6
Library of Congress Catalog Card Number 2004100245

Printed and bound in Singapore by Tien Wah Press

Half-title: Matisse drawing in the garden at Villa Le Rêve.
Title page: Matisse with his birds and flowers.
Opposite: Vase of Arum Lilies, March 1943.
Following pages: (page 6) marble-topped pedestal table in front of the studio window; (page 7) *Large Red Interior,* 1948, with the marble-topped pedestal table. Hanging on the wall are the ink drawing *Interior with Window and Palm Tree* and the painting *The Pineapple.* See photograph on page 111.

contents

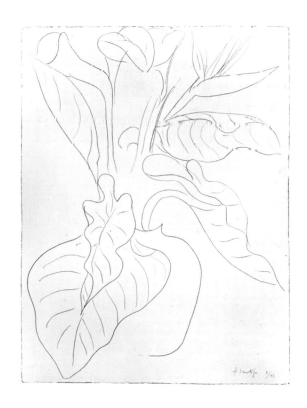

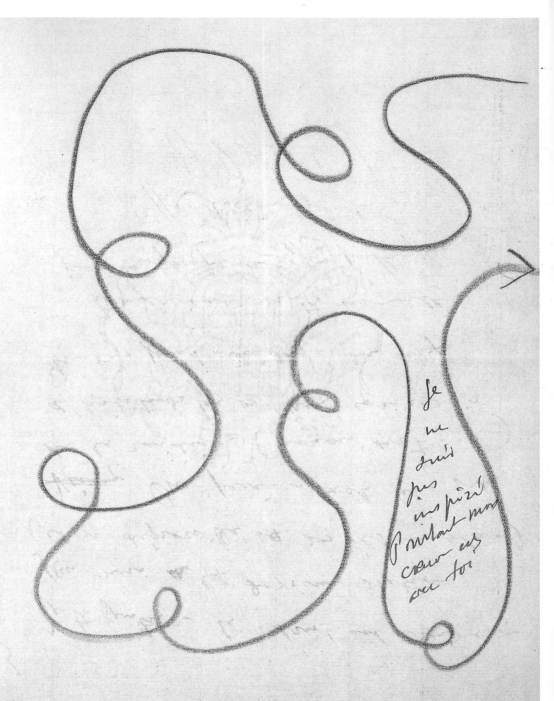

st

preface

In June 1943, with Nice under threat of Allied bombardment, Matisse took refuge for five years on the outskirts of the simple and congenial Provençal village of Vence, with nature all around him. The war was not yet over. Mme Matisse and her daughter were in Paris, where Matisse used to visit them from time to time. They had been arrested for their involvement with the Resistance, and were not released until after the liberation of Paris.

At the age of seventy-four, very famous but suffering from poor health, Matisse was living with Lydia Delectorskaya, more than forty years his junior. His model and assistant since 1935, he called her 'Mme Lydia' or 'Saint Lydia', but occasionally, if she was not at his immediate disposal, he would say she was a 'bolshevik'. She addressed him soberly as 'patron'. 'Without her, the house no longer exists,' he said simply.

Not being very mobile, he wrote almost every day to his friends, describing his family torments, his fears, the difficulties of life, his relationship with his models, with the objects around him, with his all-consuming work. Even so, as soon as he arrived there, Villa Le Rêve inspired him. He wrote to Aragon, 'Beautiful villa, and I don't mean gingerbread or pretentious. Thick walls and glass doors and windows reaching right up to the ceiling – in other words Nice light…'

In Nice, both at the Hôtel Régina and in his other studios, he had been much less in contact with nature. Rather this had been the period of windows open onto the sea. Matisse arranged for the array of objects that had followed him from studio to studio for more than forty years to be brought from Nice. These were simple, commonplace objects of no particular value, sometimes exotic artefacts he had brought back from his journeys to Morocco or Algeria, items one could see in any bourgeois household of the time: a water jug, a coffee pot, an Alsatian wine glass, brightly patterned fabrics, a wrought-iron pedestal table, ashtrays, shells, Fez pottery, Chinese porcelain, English china. And chairs, a multitude of chairs…

In the two rooms that served as his studio were a number of illustrated books, on Ronsard, Baudelaire, Montherlant and Reverdy; and the series of paintings known as the Vence interiors: *Interior in Venetian Red, Large Red Interior, The Black Fern, Interior in Yellow and Blue, Small Blue Interior, The Silence Living in Houses, Interior with an Egyptian Curtain* and *The*

Above: Self-portrait, 1947
Opposite: 'I am not inspired. Nevertheless my heart is with you' – letter to André Rouveyre, 13 December 1948

Rocaille Armchair. It was also at Le Rêve, when he was nearly eighty and having to spend more time in bed than he would have wished because of ill health, that Matisse would invent a radically new technique: he illustrated *Jazz* for the publisher Tériade with paper cut-outs that were both sumptuous and astonishing.

Fascinated by this atmosphere of poetic disorder, the photographer Hélène Adant – cousin of Lydia, and Russian, like her – was a frequent visitor at Le Rêve. From day to day she would photograph the barely discernible changes in the arrangement and combination of items that Matisse would eventually decide whether or not to paint. With a light hand, as if taking notes, she could take over twenty pictures of the same subject – such as Matisse making a charcoal sketch of a Haitian model – before, after, or during, the pedestal table with or without watermelons, with or without vases, with or without fruit, with or without the sculptor's turntable, with or without arum lilies. Some of these photographs were requested by Aragon, who was preparing a book that would not be published for almost thirty years, *Henri Matisse: A Novel*.

All these fresh, spontaneous photographs constitute a kind of 'view from the wings' on the work that is so famous today. They provide a detailed glimpse of the artist's décor right down to the last little corners of the studio where he worked. They reveal to us a sense of intimacy, and the sensual, poetic atmosphere Matisse could weave around himself. From the photographs and drawings, one can follow the trail of hesitations that would lead to the canvases – and Matisse's uninterrupted conversation with his familiar things. Like purveyors of desire or magic fetishes, they were a source of fascination for Aragon, as well as for all the other visitors, and they represented an unavoidable need for Matisse. Without them he couldn't paint. On his return to the Hôtel Régina in 1949, Matisse would once again arrange the pink shells, the pewter jug, the black fern or the rocaille armchair around him, not forgetting the red striped bergère. Until his death in 1954, he would wrap himself in the same Utopia.

I should have liked to live with some young giantess
Like a voluptuous cat at the feet of a queen.
…
I should have liked to explore her limbs at my leisure;
To climb the slope of her tremendous knees,
And sometimes when the sickly suns of summer
Made her stretch wearily across the fields,
To fall trustfully asleep in the shadow of her breasts,
Like a quiet hamlet at the foot of a mountain.

from Charles Baudelaire, 'La Géante', Les Fleurs du mal

Previous pages: Matisse in his studio at Villa Le Rêve.

Above: an extract from a letter to Aragon dated 22 August 1943:
'I have been in Vence for a month and a half and everything is fine in all respects. Beautiful landscape, on the road to Saint Jeannet, a village which always makes me think of Baudelaire's "La Géante": "To fall trustfully asleep in the shadow of her breasts, like a quiet hamlet at the foot of a mountain." '

villa le rêve

'A flower, a leaf… A glistening, shimmering stone, everything is glazed, varnished, you cannot imagine how beautiful it is… the more we look at things the less we see them.'

Raymond Escholier, Matisse ce vivant, *1956 (Eng.* Matisse from the Life, *1960)*

It was a friend of Matisse's, André Rouveyre, who found Villa Le Rêve for him. A square ochre house with brown shutters, it is an unpretentious house, built in 1930 for an English admiral on the outskirts of the village, at the foot of the rocky white 675-metre Baou mountain. Framed by three huge hundred-year-old palm trees that almost come through the windows, the villa is set in a garden full of pink laurels, yuccas, cypresses, olive trees, and all manner of abundant plants.

Matisse set up a two-room studio upstairs. He brought with him his cats, Coussi and Minouche, and a few caged doves. Since more than anything he disliked 'any persistent excesses of light',

Matisse drawing on the steps of Villa Le Rêve.

A view of the village of
Vence, taken close to the
Chapel of the Rosary,
a few hundred metres
below Villa Le Rêve.

he put up his open-work curtains at Le Rêve, like mashrabiya windows in a harem. All his collections of chairs and tables were set out in an oriental half-light, all his familiar objects, vases brimming over with flowers gathered into delightfully untidy bunches. The walls of his bedroom were hung with Polynesian tapa cloths and Kasaï textiles from the Belgian Congo. He put up recent work simply with pins on his studio walls, including the paper cut-outs. There was also his 1940 painting, *The Dream*, in which the model poses in a Romanian blouse, her head resting on her folded arms. Now Lydia – nude subject for another *Dream* in 1935 – looked after Matisse; she was muse as well as nurse and assistant. Josette, the housekeeper, took her place whenever she went out since Matisse was too frail to be left alone.

Matisse had to lead a very regular life if he wanted to work. Lydia cajoled him into a daily constitutional, and sometimes ventured as far as Nice with him in a taxi. Between sittings, he would rest and take tea with his model, but never for longer than a quarter of an hour. He would smoke a cigar, play with his cat, take a turn round the garden. Then visitors would call. Many journalists came to interview him. Photographers, such as Brassaï, Cartier-Bresson and André Ostier, were regulars, as were Aragon and Elsa Triolet. Picasso and Françoise Gilot would come up from Antibes. From the moment he was introduced to her, Matisse wanted to paint Françoise, with 'green hair' and 'a light blue colour', an idea that did not appeal to Picasso, who would himself choose to do just that a little later.

With Bonnard, who lived at Le Cannet, he shared a gentler friendship. Matisse would have liked to paint like him. There were also familiar visitors such as Henri Laurens, a great friend of Braque's, and André Rouveyre, with whom he corresponded daily and sometimes even several times a day, despite the fact that they lived in the same village. Rouveyre wrote and painted, and they had known one another since their time together at the Ecole des Beaux-Arts. Matisse never tired of discussing his work and stating his thinking to a 'select public'. His writing is always free and affectionate, full of humour and poetry, although it is also often quite sombre, and sometimes even risqué. Josette would post his letters, or deliver them by hand. She lived directly across the road from Rouveyre, above the café run by her husband. In Vence, Matisse forged links with M. Roux of the Colombe d'or, with Aimé Maeght, who was beginning to exhibit his work in Paris, and with Brother Rayssiguier, the Dominican novice with whom he discussed the decoration of the chapel just a few steps below Le Rêve.

Above: Medlar Branch, 1944
Right: Even in the garden, with his pencil in his hand, Matisse retained a certain bourgeois elegance. His shirts came from Charvet in Paris's Place Vendôme; he would wear a tie and a waistcoat, and owned a good number of hats.

'It is an area where **light plays the main role**. Colour comes second. It is with colour that you render light, although of course you must also feel this light, have it within yourself. This can happen in a very paradoxical way, but what harm can that do?'

Conversation with André Marchand, 1947

When he was not too tired, Matisse would walk the two kilometres from the villa to the main square in Vence with Lydia. He would take a taxi for the fifteen or so kilometres to Nice. *Following pages:* Villa Le Rêve and its *Phoenix canariensis* palm trees at the foot of the Baou mountain, covered in box trees, olive trees and wild holm oaks.

'I thought I was in Tahiti... When the fragrance
of woodland or burning grass is wafted on the breeze, I can smell
the wood of the islands and then I am an elephant...'

Letter to Aragon

Opposite: Vence seen from the second floor of Villa Le Rêve. *Above:* The 'Etruscan vase' often painted by Matisse.
Following pages: Villa Le Rêve with its irises and roses, palms and olive trees, and the Baou rising behind.

portrait of an armchair

Matisse was fond of chairs, and there were many in his studio at Le Rêve. Generally, in his paintings, they show a model to the best advantage. There were Voltaires (chairs with a high scrolled back), neo-Renaissance chairs in studded wood and leather, high-backed chairs covered in damask, Louis XV bergères. In the paintings one can make out the back of a chair, an armrest, a colour, the curve of a leg. In 1942, just before he moved to Vence, it was the low

'I have finally found the object I have wanted for a year. It is a Venetian baroque chair, in varnished silver, like enamel. When I saw it in an antique shop a few weeks ago, I was completely bowled over by it. It is splendid, I am smitten. With this chair I shall slowly leap up for the summer, when I am back from Switzerland.'

Letter to Aragon, 20 April 1942

Opposite: The Rocaille Armchair, 1946 and *left*, the object in real life with a coffee glass on it, filled with a few flowers.
Following pages: the letter and drawing from Matisse to Aragon, 20 April 1942, in which he describes the chair (text above).

probablet... olg'a n...

...ntré un objet pareil
Quand je l'ai rencontré
chez un autre guéri et
j'ai 99. Semaine j'ai
été complètement retour-
né — Le art splendide, j'en
suis habité, c'est avec
Qun' que je vais londri
lentement à mon rentrée
d'été — en rentrant de Suisse.

red and white striped Louis XV bergère, with large well stuffed cushions and trimmed with sophisticated piping, that was Matisse's favourite. It is to be found in *The Black Door* and *The Purple Dress* and in *Young Girl at the Window*, with creatures sitting nonchalantly in it. In the same year, however, Matisse found an eighteenth-century rocaille armchair in an antique shop in Nice, which filled him with the same enthusiasm he had felt with, say, a Romanian blouse or a mandarin's pelisse. This was not the first time he had been taken with a chair. In 1931, when he travelled to Tahiti, haunted by a canvas he had left unfinished in Nice, unsettled by a totally different light and landscape that he hoped to assimilate into his art later, disinclined to paint Tahitian women – whom he associated too closely with Gauguin's universe – he

began hastily to draw the rocking chair in his room. 'One can feel the need to gather one's thoughts before an armchair,' he wrote to Aragon. During a stay in Ciboure in 1940 he put an empty Voltaire chair in front of an open window and set it in the very centre of his painting *The Yellow Room*, having drawn it incessantly, until, as he said to Aragon in a letter, 'I was able to lift the veil on its secret'. His reaction to the rocaille chair, which he bought in 1942, was more unusual, almost like an amorous encounter: 'I was completely bowled over by it. It is splendid, I am smitten,' he wrote to Aragon.

Made up of two large silver scallop shells, for the seat and the back, with 'positively reptilian' armrests and feet reminiscent of a lizard's or the shape of sea horses, this baroque chair, brought to Le Rêve in 1943, took on the full role of a model and, with an old coffee glass on it filled with white flowers, completely invaded the *Rocaille Armchair* canvas (1946). Hélène Adant took many photographs of this chair, with and without these flowers, paired with other armchairs or seats, next to pedestal or Moorish tables, with or without printed fabrics behind it, until Matisse settled on a 'pose', as if painting the portrait of a person.

Opposite: In 1946, at Aragon's request, Hélène Adant photographed the chair, the lute and the fabric that Matisse had painted in *Tabac Royal* in 1943, shortly before he moved to Vence.
Above: The Tahitian Rocking Chair, 1931.
Following pages: the much-loved rocaille armchair, shown between two upright chairs, which Matisse would often use with loose covers for working (see pages 60 and 65).

'For me, the model is a springboard, a door that I have to break down in order to gain access to a garden where I am alone and utterly comfortable.'

Letter to Aragon

Right: In the reflection of the studio in the mirror one can just see the photographer and tripod on the left. On the wall in the far background are a pinned-up collage and the painting *Young Woman in White, Red Background*, 1946. There are two studded wood and leather chairs, of the kind seen in *Young Girl Sitting in a Persian Dress*, 1942, *above.* *Following pages:* The rocaille chair with lilies and pomegranates, next to the eighteenth-century velvet bergère (*pp. 46–47*), then with another striped bergère (*pp. 48–49*). With each 'pose' the printed background changes, evidence of Matisse's hesitation.

'One can feel the need to gather one's thoughts before an armchair… it is the tender admiration we lend to a familiar object that gives the object sufficient interest to receive a heart's overflowing.'

Letter to Aragon

Left: for *Young Woman in White, Red Background*, 1946, of which Matisse painted many versions, the chair was paired with a Tibetan pelisse covered with a tiger skin from the Gobi desert for the Congolese model who also inspired his great painting *Asia*.
Right: Shown against a Tahitian cloth, next to a bunch of asters set on the Moorish pedestal table, is the red and white striped bergère that so inspired Matisse in 1946.
Following pages: Laid out in front of the striped bergère are the plates on which Matisse is trying out the colours for a decorative scheme: a door on the theme of Leda for some South Americans.

the models' ballet

'What matters most to me?
To work my model until I have
it sufficiently within me to be
able to improvise.'

Matisse, from Gaston Diehl, Peintres d'aujourd'hui, *1943*

Nice was a cosmopolitan city in the 1940s, and Matisse
had some very varied models, often black; perhaps a
neighbour, or just as likely an unknown woman he might
have met at his antique dealer's. Some women, such as
Henriette Darricarrère when he had a studio in Place
Charles-Félix, posed for him for up to eight years
running. Others, such as 'Lorette', posed for fifty
portraits in a year. When a person interested him, he
began by observing them as they were, at rest, then he
would indicate the pose he wanted before launching
into sketches that might or might not precede a canvas.

Hélène Adant took 22 different photographs of Matisse
and his Haitian model posing for *Les Fleurs du mal*. The
rocaille armchair can be seen between them.

In that perfumed land, fondled by the sun
I knew – beneath a canopy of trees aglow with crimson,
and palms from which languor pours upon your eyes –
a Creole lady whose charms are unknown to the world.

From Charles Baudelaire, 'To a Creole Lady,' Les Fleurs du mal

'While I am working on my inspired drawings, if a model asks me the time and I pay attention, I've had it, the drawing's had it,' he wrote to Aragon. During these sessions, he would sit up close to the model, less than a metre away sometimes, with their knees touching: 'a cake in a shop window never makes you want it so much as when you go into the shop and have it right under your nose' (Lydia Delectorskaya, *Henri Matisse*, Paris 1988), he often remarked to Lydia, who would not be in the room where Matisse was working but nearby, within earshot in case he should need the slightest thing; she also met the models at the door.

Lydia kept all the clothes that inspired the artist in a special trunk. There were necklaces, furs, evening gowns, the famous Romanian blouse and the mauve Turkish kaftan he painted many times, other blouses with flounces or frills, then the big puffed Moorish trousers. Matisse would dress any model in them. The ideal woman, he often explained, was still Madame de Sennones in the Ingres painting. 'Don't move…think about the same thing,' he would say to the young Dutch refugee painter Annelies Nelck, while he was drawing her (Annelies Nelck, *L'Olivier du Rêve*). She had come to him spontaneously as a neighbour to beg for his help. Very young and restless, she was often to be seen at Le Rêve. Matisse had her pose for *Les Fleurs*

du mal, for *Leda*, and he painted her several times, notably in the Romanian blouse Lydia had worn in 1936, 1937 and 1940. He paid her generously and sent her to M. Roux of the Colombe d'or, who took an interest in young artists. One day, he even gave her the friendly gift of a small signed drawing in exchange for the bread she had brought. There was also an English girl 'with changing eyes', a Turkish woman who posed for Montherlant's *Pasiphaé*, a 14-year-old Russian girl who was the model for *Letters to a Portuguese Nun*, a smiling Haitian woman. He produced several similar canvases, *The Coat, Young Girl in a White Dress*, with the same 'gracious and charming' Congolese model, shown in a languid pose on the pelisse that was covered with a tiger skin from the Gobi desert; she had already inspired *Asia*. When he arrived at Le Rêve, Matisse was surprised to meet 'Monique B' again, the 'wonderful person' he had asked to pose for him when she was his night carer following his operation. This time it was she who was convalescing in Vence, and they quickly found themselves having *tête-à-têtes* again. She posed and made some gouaches to be used for the cut-outs. One day, when she had recovered, she told him that she was joining the Dominican convent; she eventually provided the link with the Chapel of the Rosary.

'You cannot imagine the harmonious flavour that unites her eyes, her lips and the delicate curve of her chin. I will never be able to render that. Here she is before me, like a frightened little pigeon in my hand.'

Letter to André Rouveyre, 5 April 1947

Opposite: Flawless and classical, with her short skirt and white blouse, the model, a neighbour at Le Rêve, metamorphoses into a Matissian creature thanks to a cape (*above*) or (*overleaf*) a long, flounced gown lent by Lydia, even if Matisse only needs to draw her face. Because of the cold, the model is allowed an additional electric heater and Matisse a Moroccan rug for his feet.

'Not everyone can see their interest,
it may be a **sublimated voluptousness** that
is perhaps not perceptible by everybody.'

Letter to Aragon

Above: Hair, 1944.
Left: From a letter to André Rouveyre,
8 April 1946. One of the many sketches
for the cover of *Les Fleurs du mal.*

Above: In the reflection of the mirror at the far end, Matisse and the Haitian model under the paintings *Young Woman in White, Red Background* and *Interior in Yellow and Blue*, 1946 (see page 93). The photographer's tripod is on the left. *Right:* Above Matisse's head is *Interior in Venetian Red*, 1946.

'It is a kind of flirtation ('flirt' – I would like to have
written 'fleurt'). It is as if we were to throw flowers at each other's face,
roses shedding their petals, and why not?'

Letter to André Rouveyre

Previous pages: Hélène Adant has moved around the artist and the model, whose knees are touching. Here she has her back to the window. Although he is wearing a dressing gown here, Matisse does not remove his felt hat trimmed with Tahitian raffia ribbon.
Left: the Haitian model has put on a puffed low-cut flowered blouse at Matisse's request but the checked skirt and 1940s platform shoes are her own.
Above: Berthe's Eyes, 1944, drawn for *Les Fleurs du mal*.

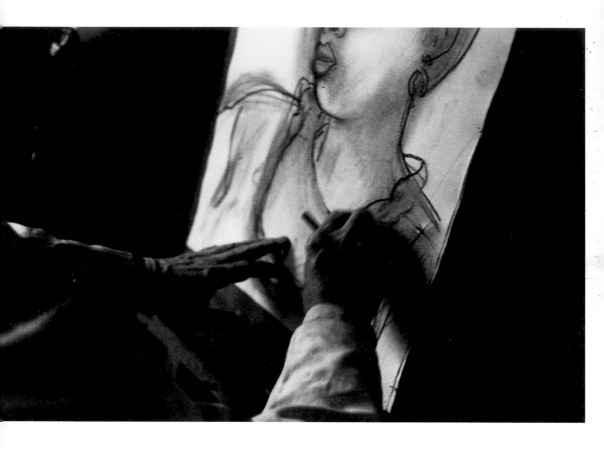

'If I trust my drawing hand it is because in training
it to serve me, I have forced myself never to let it
take precedence over my feelings.'

Matisse, Jazz

Previous pages, above and opposite: Matisse insisted on great
stillness and total silence for what he called his 'inspired drawings'.
Following pages: Once finished, the drawing would be stuck
on the wall with a pin. Posing, he is able to chat.

Her eyes fixed on me like a tame tiger,
Her look vague and dreamy, she tried out a few poses,
And a naivety mingled with lewdness
Gave a new charm to her metamorphoses.

From Charles Baudelaire, 'Les Bijoux,' Les Fleurs du mal

Orphaned at twelve years old, the Russian Lydia Delectorskaya fled Manchuria for France. In Nice, where there was a Russian colony, she began by working for Mme Matisse before helping Matisse in his studio. In Nice in 1935 she worked on *Window in Tahiti* and *Pink Nude* (photos by Matisse, *opposite and above right*). 'I wasn't his type,' she recalled in the book she wrote on the painter. Some months later, however, she posed for a series of famous paintings, including *Large Seated Nude* and *The Dream*, of which Matisse made several versions with and without the Romanian blouse. 'To be Matisse's model,' she declared in 1935, 'is to mediate between the artist and the dream'. Eight years later, in Vence, Lydia looked after the artist full-time (*above left*).

MARG.
Litho Essai
sur 45
Matisse

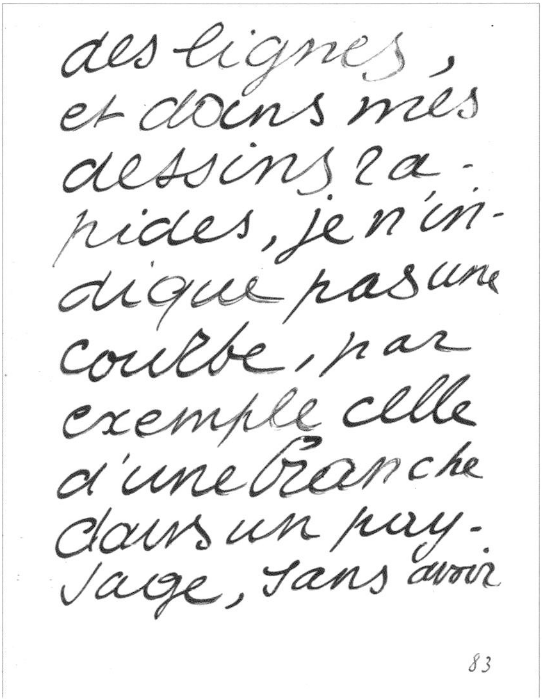

des lignes,
et dans mes
dessins ra-
pides, je n'in-
dique pas une
courbe, par
exemple celle
d'une branche
dans un pay-
sage, sans avoir

83

conscience de
son rapport
avec la verti-
cale.
Mes courbes
ne sont pas
folles.

84

Left: MARG., September 1945.
Above: from *Jazz*, pp. 83–84. 'My curves are not mad,'
wrote Matisse, whose writing and signature recall his
MARG. drawings of 1945. Recently released by the
Germans, his daughter Marguerite visited him in Vence.
He made a series of drawings of her face.

an array
of objects

'Sometimes, I pause over a motif, a
corner of my studio that I find expressive,
even it is beyond me and my strength,
and I wait for the *coup de foudre...*'

Letter to Pierre Matisse, 1 September 1940

From 1943 to 1948, Matisse did not work as effortlessly
as one might imagine. After his serious operation in 1941
he painted very little and was frequently confined to his
bed. For this reason he sought to recreate a kind of
artificial paradise around him. It was necessary for him
to feel 'The sympathy I create among the objects that
surround me, around which I live and on which I can

Arranged spontaneously by the artist or set up
according to Aragon's wishes, the still lifes in the
studio changed each time Hélène Adant called.

Objets de l'atelier de H. Matisse

467 X

468

469 X

470 X

471

472 X

473

474

475

477

480 X

82

bestow feelings of tenderness without running the risk of suffering as in real life' (letter to André Rouveyre, 6 October 1941). He therefore displayed the entire 'little collection' of printed fabrics he used as backgrounds. This was a taste that dated from his childhood, spent in northern France, at Cateau-Cambrésis, close to Bohain-en-Vermandois, a village where there were more than thirty luxury textile workshops. There was a kind of hierarchy among these objects that had evolved over time. Some of them had been the source of powerful inspiration; others made only the most fleeting appearances in his paintings. The *chocolatière* with the wooden handle, for example, was illustrated in 1906 in *Woman Reading*, then in 1909 in *Still Life with Blue Tablecloth*. The ridged pewter jug was one of his best-loved objects: it appears from 1916 and in many versions, with a glass of water and two apples on a plate or, in 1939, just before Matisse moved into Le Rêve, with lemons. In 1942, in *Still Life with a Magnolia*, it occupies a primary position. The Moorish octagonal tables, the slightly chipped blue and white china 'Tabac Royal' jar, the host of white fruit dishes, rounded Chinese blue and white vases,

long-spouted Oriental ewers and Rhineland wine glasses feature throughout his work.

It was the intensity of feeling and memories, concentrated year after year in these little objects, that Matisse sought to capture and to convey in every canvas. He was neither a collector nor an antique buff, however, which accounts for the simplicity and inexpensiveness of the objects with which he surrounded himself. As in Nice, when he was painting the odalisques, he hung his windows with openwork cotton curtains that filtered the southern light as if through a grille, covering these with a large Egyptian curtain with a vivid arabesque design. He was obsessed with the quality of the light, and the slightest thing might spoil it. He even suggested to a client who had bought a gouache from him to set up some Venetian blinds the better to enjoy it.

Aragon believed that these objects were to Matisse as words are to a poet; Matisse struggled to decide which subject to paint. He had already confided in a letter to his son Pierre in 1940, 'I am afraid of getting down to work *tête-à-tête* with objects that I have to animate myself with my feelings'. He was waiting for the *coup de foudre*.

Following pages: the array of objects that accompanied Matisse in all his studios, lined up empty and without props by Lydia, 'in order to show them to you with their personality alone', as she explained to Aragon. Chinese porcelain or opaline Fez pottery, Rhineland wine glasses, Syrian copper ewers, a pewter jug, a *chocolatière*, an earthenware jug from Saint-Omer, bowls and a fruit dish around the little statue of his friend Henri Laurens (*pp. 84–85, 86*). All these objects are easily identifiable in Matisse's paintings from the early twentieth century.

'I can only discover my art slowly – it consists of a meditation on nature, the expression of a dream, always inspired by reality.'

Conversation with Jacques Guenne

Still Life on a Table, 1941. Matisse made an enormous number of almost identical drawings before deciding whether or not to make a painting out of them. Here, at the bottom of the drawing, he has incorporated his own hand with his pencil and paper.

Henri Matisse 41

The *chocolatière*, the jug, the shells and the table photographed in 1946 were the subject of the 1940 painting *Still Life with Shells on Black Marble*. This *chocolatière* had already been the star of *Woman Reading* in 1906 and *Still Life with Blue Tablecloth* in 1909. *Opposite:* The ridged pewter jug, photographed with a shell, features in many paintings, including *The Pewter Jug*, 1916.

The ridged pewter jug is photographed above with
elements that are reproduced in the drawing (*right*) and
in the painting *Still Life with a Magnolia*, 1941, painted
just before Matisse's arrival at Villa Le Rêve.
Right: Themes and Variations (G1),
December 1941–January 1942.
Left: Shell.

'Drawing counts for a lot and it is also the expression of how we possess objects. When you know an object thoroughly you can invest it with an exterior trait that will define it altogether.'

Matisse, from Gaston Diehl, Problèmes de la peinture, *1945*

Below: In *Interior in Yellow and Blue*, as in *Interior in Venetian Red*, both painted in 1946, we see the same interplay of the marble-topped pedestal table, the rocaille chair and the Fez pottery with the two watermelons. However, the photographs (*left, and on following pages 94–95, 96–97*) show how the details surrounding these central elements change all the time.

'The object is not so interesting in itself. It is the surroundings that create the object. This is how I have worked all my life, in front of the same objects that have given me the strength of reality by involving my spirit in all that these objects had been through for me and with me. A glass of water with a flower is something different from a glass with a lemon.'

Commentaries collected by Maria Luz, XXème siècle no. 2, January 1952, and approved by Matisse

Some fatsia leaves have appeared on the table, and some fragrant rose geraniums suddenly fill the church vase, while the sculptor's turntable and the pewter jug have disappeared. The 'Tabac Royal' jar is now in the foreground. The Moroccan rug that warmed Matisse's feet on page 60 is rolled up in the corner.

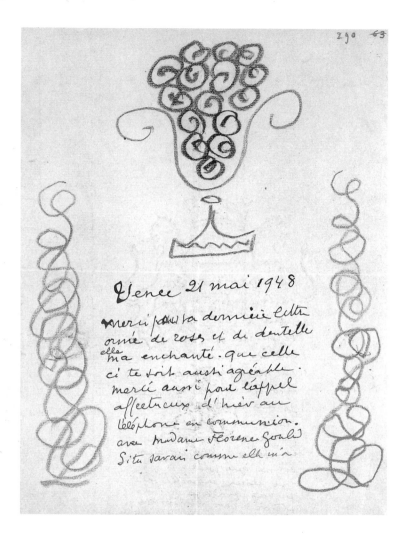

The red cotton oriental openwork curtains that recall the Moroccan Haiti scenes appear in several of the odalisque canvases dating from this period. They filter the light. But it is the halo of feelings and memories surrounding an object that explains Matisse's faithfulness to it. *Above:* Letter to André Rouveyre, 21 May 1948: 'Thank you for your last letter decorated with roses and lace, which I found delightful'. These two almost octogenarian gentlemen were certainly not embarrassed to show their mutual affection.

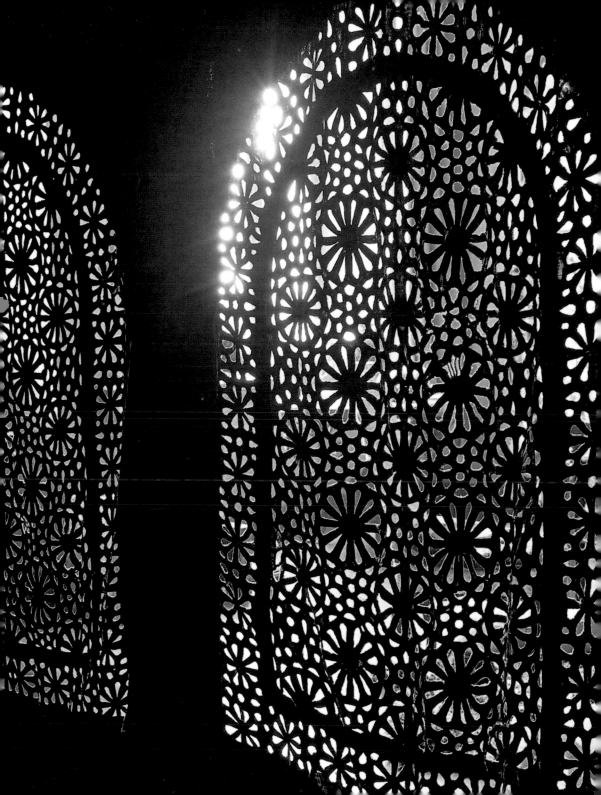

'nature accompanies me, exalts me...'

One day, getting ready to leave for Paris, Matisse wrote to Aragon: 'I am leaving here on the seventh with some regret because I see nature in all her beauty, and all the hardiness and ardour of the plants… In Paris, I shall find a landscape made of stone.' At Le Rêve, Matisse drew many trees, leaves and flowers because he walked through his garden every day, watched it from the window, took strolls around it, rested in it: 'I have just taken my nap under an

'I would not get rid of my feelings by copying the tree exactly or by drawing the leaves one by one in the current idiom… Only after I have identified myself with it. I have to create an object that resembles the tree. The symbol of the tree.'

Letter to Aragon

Opposite: Interior with Egyptian Curtain, 1948. After the discovery of the tomb of Tutankhamun by Lord Carnarvon in 1922, these heavy, multicoloured appliqué Qanat wall-hangings became fashionable.

olive tree and the colour and softness of what I saw was deeply moving. It seems that this a paradise and that one should not analyse it…' (letter to Charles Camoin, 23 May 1918). Trees may have been his favourite. When he looked at them or painted them, he wavered constantly between passion and mastery. 'I would be so taken with the beauty of the trunk, its power and its mystery, that I could get no further than its main branches' (letter to André Rouveyre). During his convalescent walks, he might pick up a medlar branch, an olive bough, three cosmos flowers, some grasses or an iris… 'I came back to the house with the idea of painting these flowers once I had arranged them in my own way, but what a disappointment, all their charm is lost in this arrangement, what happened?' (*Jazz*). An involuntary order had replaced the casual appearance and the pleasure behind what he had picked, and Matisse decided there and then that Josette, the housekeeper, should be the only person to arrange flowers. From that moment on a daily harvest of all the plant varieties gleaned from the market in Vence, from the roadside or from the garden, marked the ritual passing of time from season to season. The tables in the studio were covered with a joyous, untidy, artless accumulation that recalled the altars for Corpus Christi in June in the French countryside. And so the magic would work its wonders: 'I put some flowers on the table and I wish, once the paintings are finished, that a gardener could recognize all the varieties of flowers they contain, but I don't know what happens along the way, they end up becoming young girls dancing' (letter to Aragon). Sometimes, he would think of a flower which he would immediately want to 'identify with', as he put it, and he would telephone his florist in Nice. So when he ordered hyacinths one day, he asked Aragon to bring forward his planned visit because afterwards he 'would be unable to think of anything else' and would not want to see anyone. Roses were the only flowers that intimidated him, and he drew very few of them 'because first one has to forget all the roses that have ever been painted.'

When winter drew near and flowers became scarce Matisse turned to a shrivelled old plane tree leaf, an asparagus stem, or humble little ivy flowers like starry, mustard-coloured pompoms. After this, when he began illustrating *Jazz* with his paper cut-outs, it was the sea, and – more than fifteen years after his journey to Tahiti – the memory of leisurely swims in the lagoons that engulfed him. 'I would swim around the colours of the corals, emphasized by the sharp, black tones of the sea cucumbers…' In the tranquillity of Vence, he was able to paint Polynesia at last.

Composition with Standing Nude and Black Fern, 1948. When he lived in Nice, Matisse saw palm trees from his window overlooking the sea. Here at Le Rêve the three enormous *Phoenix canariensis*, with their plumed foliage (*following pages*), almost touch the house; inside ferns and philodendrons take over from them.

'I have wanted to draw trees so many times but I've never managed it. In my first attempts, trying to copy, I have never been encouraged to go on with the drawing, since the result would be lifeless, without making any connection with the feeling that encouraged me to draw the tree. Then, when I would try for nothing but my feeling, my emotion, I would be so taken with the beauty of the trunk, its power and its mystery, that I could get no further than its main branches…'

Letter to André Rouveyre

Left: The Silence Living in Houses, 1947, is also the portrait of an olive tree whose 'limbs' reminded Matisse of those of a mammoth. In a letter dated 1 May 1947 *(following pages)* entitled 'Desolation', Matisse confided to Rouveyre his sadness at the plane trees along the avenues in Vence having been pruned, 'dishonoured' as he saw it, and what was more, there were no more shadows.

Vence, "La désolation" – 1er Mai '47

Cher Rouveyre –

J'ai découvert ce matin pourquoi je me suis trouvé si seul à Vence à mon arrivée – voici :

tous les arbres ont été élagués – quand je dis élagués je pourrai dire deshonorés – c'est ainsi que tous les platanes des avenues sont réduits à ceci. et encore mon maladroit dessin peut encore passer pour évoquer une main – mais les platanes ici n'ont plus d'aucune analogie avec ce qui nous est familier.

J'ai déjà su faire des choses analogues à Nice où on laissait à l'arbre au sommet une seule branche pour faire un appel de sève –

Mais ici plus rien donc
plus d'ombre. Que vais-
je te dire toi à ton colombier
les avenues de Venee —
la place du grand jardin.
C'est comme si la
bombe atomique avait
aspiré tout ce qu'il y a.
Pour ne pas être en retard
mon Harett à part la
même chose — de beaux
oliviers.

Madame de
Mme olivier [...]
camarade !

Above: Letter to André Rouveyre, 10 January 1946.
Illustration for 'Pavot d'or', a poem written by Roger Bernard,
a disciple of René Char and member of the Resistance who
had been shot in 1944. Matisse wanted to help his widow.
Right: Matisse attends to his flowers. Recognizable on the
wall are *The Pineapple* (1948), the ink drawing *Interior with
Window and Palm Tree* (1948), and part of the painting
Still Life with Pomegranates (1947).

Left: Interior with Window and Palm Tree, 1948, which gave its name to a painting of the same name, and, *below, Bouquet of Hellebores,* 1943–44, in a Saint-Omer blue and white earthenware vase. *Following pages:* The procession of flower models, whose portraits Matisse was to paint. He drew them with the same delicate sensuality, even the simplest of them. Arum lilies, tulips, narcissi, irises, peach blossom, phlox, lilacs, anemones, nasturtiums, pinks, lily-of-the valley, roses, zinnias, gladioli, magnolia flowers, camellias, dahlias, soapworts, hyacinths and hellebores, but also ferns, grasses, ivy flowers, fatsias, philodendrons, fig leaves, brambles and even seaweed… all are clearly identifiable.

'What soft and tender
light despite its brightness!
I don't know why I often think of
it in the same way as the light of
Touraine. In Touraine it is a little
more golden. Here it is silvery.'

Letter to Charles Camoin, 23 May 1918

The *Monstera deliciosa* philodendron leaves with their cut-out
shapes are placed in front of the window to create some shade.
They already featured in *The Guitarist* in 1930 and in most of
the nudes of Lydia painted in 1935 or 1936.

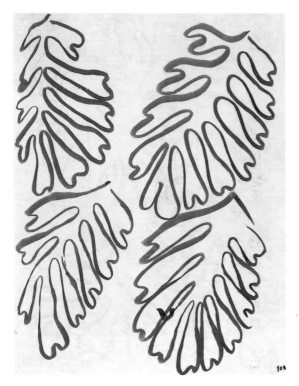
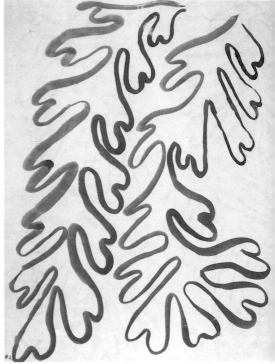

Above: Ink-drawings in a letter to André Rouveyre,
dated 8 April 1946.
Opposite: The leaves of the philodendron were easily
transformed into seaweed for the illustrations for
Lagoon, 1944, with paper cut-outs for *Jazz*.